By Mikal Lofgren

Poems for My Eve

LEAVENING: Humor from our General Authorities

SALT: Humor and Wisdom from Brigham Young

WHEAT

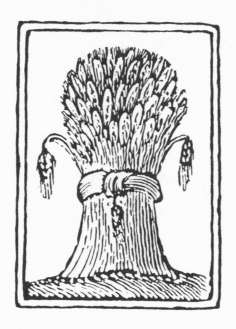

Humor & Wisdom
of J. Golden Kimball

Mikal Lofgren

Moth House Publications
3967 South 2200 West
Salt Lake City, Utah 84119

Library of Congress Catalog Card Number: 80-81556
ISBN 0-936718-04-8

For Bruce and Audrey
Whose friendship bridges the miles.

PREFACE

In his own lifetime J. Golden Kimball became a folk hero who had amusing tales told of himself throughout the Church. He is now perhaps most famous as the general authority humorist who swore at the altar, but this narrow view of his life slights the real value of the man.

J. Golden Kimball was probably more than anything a man of deep and abiding faith. He had a wide range of experience from which he gained the down-to-earth wisdom evidenced in his talks. At the age of fifteen, after the death of his father, Heber C. Kimball, he began supporting his mother, brother, and sister. Times were hard and often the anticipated results of the hard work were not seen, but J. Golden got experience, and from that experience he gleaned the wisdom that enabled him to speak in the down-to-earth manner which endeared him to the members of the Church.

J. Golden, a lean whipcord of a man often compared to Will Rogers and Mark Twain, used humor to tweak the saints and to touch them in a human way where they were most tender.

Perhaps most fundamental to his capturing the interest of his audience was the lack of distance between himself and his listeners. He did not erect a facade of perfection between himself and the lay members but spoke directly and forthrightly of not only their problems but his own. I am convinced that it was this speaking from the heart that so endeared him to the members of his time because in speaking from his heart he spoke directly to their hearts.

I find this so even today as I re-read his conference speeches. J. Golden Kimball speaks to my heart, and so this *Wheat* gleaned from his talks.

CONTENTS

I realize, my brethren and sisters, that, during the past thirty years I may have said some foolish things. I have in my own way, given the people a good deal of chaff to get them to take a little wheat, but some of them haven't got sense enough to pick the wheat out from the chaff.

J. Golden Kimball

Conference Report. October, 1921, p. 83.

AGENCY

I am very doubtful if a man can be saved in the kingdom of God who has no individuality, and does not assert his agency, because salvation is an individual work.

Conference Report. April, 1907, p. 78.

Now, as I said, I waived certain rights when I became a member of this Church; I waived the right of sin. I had my agency and individuality; but as long as I am a member of this Church, I waive the right to sin, to transgress. When you joined the Church, became members of it, you also waived the right to do a great many things. You have no right to break the ten commandments, have you? You have no right to be dishonest. You have waived all these rights. You have waived the right to break the Word of Wisdom. And in many other things we have waived our rights, and sometimes I feel muzzled when I wrestle with my nature and human weaknesses. You know there is no other man just like me in all Israel, and probably you are glad of it. I am having a pretty hard time wrestling with myself. I don't feel self-righteous; I feel more like that poor fellow who stood on the street corner and bowed his head and said, "O God, forgive me, a poor sinner."

Conference Report. April, 1907, p. 80.

14

I feel a good deal, or at least I imagine I do, like a man does when held up by a burglar and he is looking into the muzzle of a six-shooter. I would quietly and willingly hold my hands up, but during the time would think of what I would do if given my liberty. We are in a similar position today, but all the men in the United States cannot prevent a man from thinking. There are not Apostles enough in the Church to prevent us from thinking, and they are not disposed to do so; but some people fancy because we have the Presidency and Apostles of the Church they will do the thinking for us. There are men and women so mentally lazy that they hardly think for themselves. To think calls for effort, which makes some men tired and wearies their souls. Now, brethren and sisters, we are surrounded with such conditions that it requires not only thought, but the guidance of the Holy Spirit. Latter-day Saints, you must think for yourselves. No man or woman can remain in this Church on borrowed light.

Conference Report. April, 1904, p. 28.

APPEARANCES

When I look over this body of men, I do not discover that you are very distinguished in appearance. Why, you are no better looking than I am, and I look pretty bad.

Conference Report. October, 1910, p. 34.

How could he tell from the outside of a man whether he has religion, or, call it faith in God and in the gospel of Jesus Christ? That can only be discovered by the life we lead and by the spirit that is within us.

Conference Report. October, 1924, p. 70.

ATTITUDE

Brethren and sisters, when I am satisfied everybody is satisfied. I can see a hole in a doughnut. I have always grieved of a doughnut. My mother was a doughnut maker. When she showed me those doughnuts, I grieved over the hole. Some of the people say there is no hole in a doughnut, but I never could agree with them. I always see the hole and forget about the doughnut.

Conference Report. April, 1921, p. 181.

"Rock-a-bye baby in the tree top" won't work out our problems. There is no use crying "All is well in Zion," because it is not true.

Conference Report. October, 1912, p. 27.

Have you ever read Coue's book? When I was sick, I

read it from lid to lid, and I went trotting around, saying: "Every day, in every way, I am getting better and better." Every morning when I got up I was worse and worse.

Conference Report. April, 1926, p. 61.

BUSINESS

What is a good man? That has been a big problem with me. I have had a good deal of business dealings with men who claimed to be good men. They said they were good and they told me how good they were, and when they got through with me I did not have anything left. Whenever a man comes to me now and tells me how honest he is, how good he is, I am not going to do business with him.

Conference Report. October, 1932, p. 18.

When I think of my father, who had his inheritance, owned the land where most of the Capitol grounds are and away off to the left, I remember that he took these poor English people that have emigrated from Europe, and took them up on the hill, showed them a lot, and asked them if they would build a home, and they said they would, and it cost them $2.50! Heber C. Kimball and the brethren never speculated and made money off the people.

Conference Report. April, 1927, p. 57.

I have been in business of different kinds; I have been a farmer, a stock raiser, a real estate man, and an implement man, but I never had one of the Apostles, or any one of the Presidency of the Church, interfere or even give me any advice or counsel in all those years of business. The only thing I am sorry for is that I didn't have sense enough to ask advice.

Conference Report. October, 1904, p. 58.

All the investments I ever made in my life, except the one of two Liberty Bonds I have been able to pay for, at four per cent, I have paid from eighteen percent down, and all I got out of it was experience; the other fellow got my money.

Conference Report. October, 1918, p. 31.

One of my brethren said to me—and he is a man so kind and gentle that I had every reason to believe he would extend to me a little sympathy—I told him of one of my last speculations and he said "If you are as big a sucker as that you ought to take your medicine." I said: "I am taking it, and it is not sugar-coated either."

Conference Report. October, 1931, p. 57.

CALLINGS

I do not think as a people we have any special use for presidents of stakes, or bishops of wards, who are not directed by inspiration. Without the guidance of the Holy Spirit we cannot fill our appointments.

Conference Report. April, 1923, p. 125.

And I say to you that some of you—and I may be among that number—place too much stress upon the positions that men hold in the Church, and we fancy in our weakness that we cannot be saved, that we cannot serve God, that we cannot be faithful and true and enjoy revelation from God, unless we have high office in the Church. There is danger in exalted position, and where "much is given much is required." The poorest man in all Israel, though he may carry a hod and be dressed like a pauper, is entitled to revelation from God, and he is entitled to lay hands on the sick, and they shall recover through the prayer of faith.

Conference Report. April, 1901, p. 51.

It is marvelous in my sight how men that are called by divine authority increase in wisdom and knowledge, how they progress, and how well they fill their positions when they have the spirit of their office and calling.

Conference Report. April, 1902, p. 8.

I claim that every man fills his niche when he is called of God and set apart and ordained to an office. He may not fill it in the way someone else would fill it, but if he is a man of courage he will fill it in his own way, under the influence of the Holy Spirit.

Conference Report. October, 1937, p. 31.

CHILDREARING

A lot of us boys used to meet up in the Eighteenth ward, right where now stands the Lafayette school—that beautiful building which cost over $170,000. I was educated in a very small building on the same block. We had a brother that was somewhat of a general, and he trained us boys—that is, when father was away. He would get us behind the barn, where no one could see us; then he would put a chip upon one of our shoulders and tell one of the other boys to knock it off, then we would fight. That was part of the training he gave us, and when we asked why he did it, he said it makes you tough. My father had a great garden and it was fenced in by a six or eight foot stone wall. Father told us we couldn't have any of the fruit, so we got it anyhow, and I will tell you how we got it. This same brother of ours, took one of the boys and dangled him over the wall with a rope, and he loaded his shirt bosom and pockets with apples. One time, Father Tucker, the gardener, got after him with a willow, and lambasted him. Brother said that would make him tough. Now, I have a little boy—my oldest son—and when he was a child we always made him give up to every neighbor's boy that came in our home. These are parables that I am telling you now. We kept that up until he thought he had to give up everything in the world, and it made rather a coward out of him. He went to school, and the boys found out they could whip him; and they did so, until I told him that if he didn't take his own part and fight, I would whip him. Not long ago he came home with his thumb out of joint, and, forgetting all about my religion, I said, Did you whip him? He said, yes.

19

Conference Report. April, 1905, p. 53.

I love God for one thing, if nothing else, that He gives to every one of His children, black or white, bond or free, an equal chance. I like equality of opportunity, and whenever parents make a favorite of a child, I feel sorry for the favorite. If you want to destroy your family show favoritism, and do not give every child an equal chance.

Conference Report. April, 1913, p. 87.

I recall that the first thing these great men did, President Brigham Young and his followers, was to select their inheritances. Heber C. Kimball had the privilege of taking one of these city blocks. And now his posterity are a race of people that we think numbers more than two thousand. He went up on the hill, dug the rocks out, and built a stone wall around the block. And I was kept inside of it on Sundays. And I hate rock walls yet!

Conference Report. April, 1927, p. 53.

My heart has not been broken yet over my children, but I realize the danger; and whenever one of my boys goes away I am concerned; I am full of anxiety, I have little peace or rest of body. All in the world I can do with my boy, my oldest boy, who is away now at work, because I cannot get him work here—and that is a responsibility resting upon us, to provide employment here for our boys and girls, so that we won't have to send them away off; we should regard that as a part of our religion;—all in the world I can do for my boy is to teach him good principles. I do a great deal of writing, and I just put a little good counsel in here and there, and hope he will catch it, and get his feet anchored, and realize the danger that menaces him on every side.

Conference Report. April, 1913, p. 85.

I have only one ambition, viz., to follow in the footsteps of my father and emulate his example.

Conference Report. October, 1898, p. 17.

CHRIST

The more we think of and study Christ's way of living and preaching the more we are impressed that there was a lack of fixed formalities or haste in his plan of work.

There were no false standards of time, no statistics, no wrong estimates of the great importance of numbers. His mission was to minister to seeking hearts anywhere and at any time. The only time, so far as we know, that Jesus excluded himself was when he went aside alone to pray.

How strikingly in contrast with our modern conception of the value of time, and of organization, and of efficiency, which so completely fills our days with one pressing engagement after another, running hither and thither, until we have little or no time to minister to the needy, the hungry, the naked, the disconsolate ones who are ever with us. It would almost seem that materialism and selfishness and greed have nearly driven out of us that Christlike spirit.

Conference Report. April, 1934, p. 32.

Remember, I pray you, that our Savior did not wait for his children to come to him. He went to them. If they were hungry, he fed them. If they were sick, he healed them. If they were in sorrow, he comforted them. If they were ignorant, he taught them. If they were distressed, he encouraged them. If they were burdened with sin, he proclaimed to them his Father's forgiveness, if they would repent and sin no more.

Conference Report. October, 1933, p. 44.

In thinking about the mission of our Savior, I desire to give a little evidence for my faith in God the Father and in His Son, Jesus Christ. I love the Lord because of His great patience. When I think of His patience in creating this world in which we live, which they claim took six thousand years, that of itself appeals to me. When I think of the patience of the Father and His Son with me, one of His children; how, through His providence, His

care and protection, and the whisperings of the Holy
Spirit, that I have been able to do as well as I have, I feel
to thank Him for His kindness unto me. Sometimes, I
marvel that I have done as well as I have.

Conference Report. October, 1910, p. 31.

COMMITMENT

When it comes to self-sacrifice, fighting for truth, they
are like the dying man who was asked by the minister,
"Will you denounce the devil and all his workings?" The
dying man looked up in a feeble and distressed way and
said, "Please don't ask me to do that. I am going to a
strange country, and I don't want to make any
enemies."

Conference Report. October, 1912, p. 27.

The Lord knows if there is any one I sympathize with
it is a man who is not doing his duty and who is a member of this Church, because I know how he feels. I am
going to tell you how he feels, because I know whereof I
speak. I have been in that place, in the history of my life.

"A man who considers his religion a slavery has not
begun to comprehend the real nature of religion. To such
men, religion is a life of crosses and mortifications. They
find their duty unpleasant and onerous. It is to them a
law of restraint and constraint. They are constantly op-
pressed with what they denominate 'a sense of duty.' It
torments them with a consciousness of their inefficiency
and with a multiplied perplexing doubt of the
genuineness of their religious experiences. They feel
themselves enchained within the bounds of a religious
system." That is the feeling of every man who is
careless, and every man who is indifferent. Are they

happy in that condition? I say no; only those are happy who are doing their duty.

Conference Report. April, 1911, p. 70.

I now ask you in all solemnity, brethren—and you might as well look the cannon in the mouth; as this is no Sunday School proposition when you talk about preaching the Gospel—don't we know, haven't we been? I know something about it; I have filled two missions. I don't look like I would ever be able to go again, but I am ready. I hardly think I could pass a physical examination, but my temperature is all right, and my pulse is beating regularly, and I am ready to face the music. I have enough faith to accept a call.

Conference Report. April, 1915, p. 134.

23

I remember reading a story. The incident happened during the civil war, when a large committee of Christian ministers came to Washington to wait on President Abraham Lincoln. After they had performed their duties, one of the Christian ministers turned to President Lincoln, and he said, "I hope the Lord is on our side." That is what all these nations are hoping, that the Lord is on their side. And President Lincoln said, "Well, I am not much concerned about that. What I am most concerned about is whether we are on the Lord's side."

Conference Report. October, 1917, p. 134.

COVENANTS

Now the point I want to reach if I can, if the Lord will give men his Spirit, is just this: Heber C. Kimball made the following statement which deeply impressed me:

"I would that all men and women who enter these holy temples could be made to understand that we are placed under obligations to God." Whenever we are permitted to enter the holy temples and perform those ordinances "We make covenants with the Father, the Son and the Holy Ghost."

Conference Report. April, 1931, p. 88.

I desire to refer back to a time when I was about thirteen years of age, when Heber C. Kimball sent word to my brother, Joseph Kimball, who is now in the Church Office Building, and myself, to come to his office. When we arrived there, mere boys, he said to us: "If you want your father's blessing you be at the endowment house in the morning and have your endowments."

Of course we were frightened nearly to death. I do not know how people feel when they are going to be executed, but that is the sort of feeling I had, not knowing and having no conception of what it all meant. However, we were there and we had our endowments. I did not remember much of that which transpired, but I was awed, and the impression was burned into my soul of the sacredness of that place, and the sacredness of the covenants which I had entered into when almost a child. When I was fifteen years old our father passed away, and we were left as many children are to wander up and fight our battles as best we could.

Conference Report. April, 1931, pp. 87-88.

If you want to be popular, stop doing the things that I have mentioned, and deny their truth. But if you want to stay with this Church, be true to your covenants. The time will come when you will be—as you are now—a light set upon a hill. I tell you, all the devils in hell cannot destroy this Church. And the devil never has been entirely comfortable since that temple [the Salt Lake Temple] was completed.

Conference Report. April, 1903, p. 32.

Now I want to prophesy, as the son of a prophet, that if this people want to be blessed they must labor for Zion; for if you labor for money you shall perish. You are under covenant, and it is a demand that God makes of this people that they redeem Zion. You have got to be generous, and you have got to place all that you have and are upon the altar and learn to live the law of the celestial kingdom.

Conference Report. April, 1898, p. 44.

CRITICISM

If you can handle your own home, and mind your own business, you will have no time for fault-finding.

Conference Report. April, 1913, p. 90.

The question always arises in my mind as to whether we joined the Church of Jesus Christ of Latter-day Saints or joined ourselves to the presiding officers. I remember hearing related a story of one of our brethren being very severely reproved by President Brigham Young, and afterwards said: "Now go and apostatize." The reply came back,"I will never do it, this is not your Church but the Church of Jesus Christ of Latter-day Saints."

We must each and every one of us have this lesson indelibly impressed upon us, and cease troubling ourselves outside of those things for which we are responsibile.

Conference Report. October, 1901, p. 55.

I will tell you a great truth which is "To know thyself, oh man," and then let the other fellow alone. One of the good sisters said to me, "Golden if you wouldn't talk so much about yourself, it would be a good thing." Well, I thought to myself, it would be a good thing if you would talk about yourself and let other people alone. I know more about myself than any other person on earth, and I am going to try to keep some of it quiet, if I can.

Conference Report. April, 1909, pp. 36-37.

26

I desire to inform you that men and women that are not keeping the commandments of the Lord, but are continually giving way to their weaknesses, justify themselves by pointing out what they consider mistakes in the presiding officers of the Church. They worry very much more about something that does not come under their supervision than they do about their transgressions.

Conference Report. October, 1901, p. 55.

I sustain and uphold, with all my heart and soul, President Heber J. Grant as the prophet of God. It was only two months ago that a young lawyer—I suppose he considers himself one of the brilliant young lawyers—undertook to criticize severely the President of the Church. I was somewhat disturbed. I said, "I am going to take out my watch and give you five minutes to name a better man." I haven't heard from him yet.

Conference Report. April, 1930, p. 61.

DEATH

I am not disposed to talk about death—to me it is a

gruesome subject; I am willing to try to encourage the other fellow, but I cannot get much happiness out of it for myself.

Conference Report. April, 1935, p. 35.

You will be surprised how I will moderate in the next ten years; I will be as mild as a summer's morn, because I will commence then to look for death. But I expect to live a number of years yet, and I hope the fire won't entirely burn out of me. I had one of the Apostles tell me, "Brother Kimball, if you don't quit making so much noise, you will burn out." "Well," said I, "I want to burn out, and give room for somebody else, as I believe some men live too long."

Conference Report. April, 1902, p. 9.

I have no fear of the hereafter. I am not afraid of God. I know God is a God of love, a Father who will look after you, if you will trust him.

Conference Report. April, 1927, p. 55.

When I came in the Tabernacle yesterday afternoon, I was met by one of my old missionary friends. He said, "Hell, Golden, I thought you were dead." Now, I want to notify my friends, and I have some good friends—I have tested them out, I know—not to worry about me; that when I am dead—and it is an awful job to get there, I have found that out, when I die, I have made arrangements for a brass band.

Conference Report. April, 1921, p. 178.

DEBT

An honest man is in hell when he is in debt. I know all about the feeling.

Conference Report. October, 1931, p. 56.

I am very much interested in the financial welfare of this people, because I realize from my own experience that when men are in financial difficulties, and their honesty is in question, and they are unable to fulfill their agreements, it is very difficult for honest men who are sensitive to the reproach of the children of men to feel joyous and happy, and to appreciate the blessings with which they are surrounded. I want to say to you that the sun does not shine brightly to such men, the grass is not green, and sometimes I fancy, they hardly feel that water runs down hill. It is a most terrible condition to be in.

Conference Report. April, 1898, pp. 42-43.

I met a banker a few weeks ago—we were very friendly. Thank the Lord, I do not owe that bank anything, but I owe another bank. I said: "How are things going?"

"Well, we are taking everything but their suspenders."

I thought afterwards that I should have said to him; If that bank hasn't got any more elasticity than my suspenders, I will throw them in.

Conference Report. October, 1931, p. 57.

I was up in Smithfield at a conference, and I preached to the people on the subject of debt. . . .and there was a salesman at this meeting. I saw him the other day at one of the conference meetings. That made me think of it. He was a salesman of the Co-operative Wagon and Machine Company. After I preached my discourse I met this man and he said: "Brother Kimball, that is the best sermon I ever heard. I never sold as many implements in my life as I did after you preached that sermon." After I had warned the people and forewarned them, that to be in debt was to be in hell—I don't know anything about hell, but that is the worst hell I have ever been in—to be in debt. I can tell you how you can keep out of debt; but I can't tell you how to get out after you get in.

Conference Report. October, 1921, p. 85.

EARTH

You good people and parents living on your farms in the country, I plead with you not to send your children to cities, where the beautiful spirit of things God created perishes. Let them live in the open, in the beautiful valleys, on the mountains, in God's sunshine, near streams, rivers, and trees and let his Spirit teach them of the things of God.

Conference Report. October, 1937, p. 34.

If this earth is to be your heaven, I think you had better have an inheritance here, don't you? I do not believe the doctrine for one minute that you people, or myself (and I think I am as good as some of you), are going immediately after death to the arms of Jehovah. It will take some of us a long time to get there. You had better be very good and take care of this earth.

Conference Report. October, 1906, p. 118.

ELECTION

My father said that his election had been made sure, and just before his death an angel appeared to him and told Heber C. Kimball, "Your work is finished." His work was completed, his election was made sure. We don't hear much about that now-a-days.

Conference Report. April, 1923, p. 128.

ENDURING

I thought I would like to read some scripture as a closing of my remarks: I am sure I can make it in two minutes. It is something my father read, in reading from his old Book of Mormon, that was published or printed in 1830. I found this page worn almost out, and I wondered what it was. This is what I found. It was just such a condition that we are now in. They had had a war, and they had had famine, and then they went to the prophet and appealed to the Lord, so that the famine was withdrawn, and it says: "That ended the eighty and fifth year." In thirteen years that people fell down two or three times, and yet they were God's people. This is what he said. I want to read it to you and impress you, if I can, with this one thought: "And thus we can behold how false and also the unsteadiness of the hearts of the children of men; yea, we can see the Lord in his great infinite goodness doth bless and prosper those who put their trust in him. Yea, and we may see at the very time when he doth prosper his people, yea, in the increase of their fields, their flocks and their herds, and in gold, and in silver, and in all manner of precious things of every kind and art; sparing their lives, and delivering them out of the hands of their enemies; softening the hearts of their enemies that they should not declare wars against them; yea, and in fine, doing all things for the welfare and happiness of his people; yea then is the time," —Now that strikes me as a strange thing. After God has done all that for his children, and it could not be written any better if it was written of this people, how God had blessed them—"then is the time that they do harden their hearts, and do forget the Lord their God and do trample under their feet the Holy One—yea, and this because of their ease, and their exceedingly great prosperity.

"And thus we see that except the Lord doth chasten his people with many afflictions, yea, except he doth visit them with death and with terror and with famine and with all manner of pestilence, they will not remember him."

We are just like all other children of God, in all other dispensations. Notwithstanding the fact that we are a chosen people, for a special purpose, our hearts have been hardened and we have forgotten our God—some of us.

Conference Report. October, 1921, pp. 85-86.

Now I grant, my brethren and sisters, that sometimes we have to endure, and I presume that if we live the Gospel of the Lord Jesus Christ we have to endure all things; but it requires a very prayerful heart to enable us to endure some things.

Conference Report. April, 1905, p. 53.

In conclusion I will tell you a story, and then will close. When I was in California I was very low spirited and broken down in body; and I tried to die, but I made a miserable failure of it. One day when I was laying on the sand, near the ocean, I happened to pick up a paper, and it gave me new life and new energy. It was a funny picture; it was a picture of a great big monkey, it represented "Fate—the Old Monkey." It was an editorial. I haven't it with me, but I have read it a good many times, and I desire to make a comparison. There was a very prominent citizen that had an intelligent monkey. He was a mischievous fellow, and he just went around the house knocking everything down that he could get hold of. He knocked over everything that he came to; he discovered that the things he knocked over did not get up again. He was just as mischievous as fate seems to be with us. Finally, this good citizen took the image of a little man, made of some kind of material, and placed it on a very strong base. It was so arranged that when you knocked it over it would come up again. So he set this little man in the room. The monkey came around, took his right hand and cuffed it over. To his surprise it wobbled a little and staggered, and then rose up and seemingly looked at him. Then he took his other hand and cuffed it again, and it came up again. Then he took the hand of his right leg and knocked it again, and then with his left hind leg; then he got on it with all four hands and took one hand up at a time. To his surprise the little man rose up. The intelligent monkey almost became a monkey maniac. He kept at it and kept at it until he hated and despised the little man; and whenever they would move the little man near the monkey, he would get off in the corner and chatter and become angry. He wouldn't have anything to do with the little man. The Church of Jesus Christ of Latter-day Saints is similar, or like that little man. You can knock it down one thousand times; it may wobble, but it will rise up again, and it will keep rising up until God has accomplished His work.

Conference Report. October, 1910, pp. 34-35.

FAITH

In conclusion: You good people learn to love God. But without faith what can you do? All of us can have faith, and without it we cannot accomplish a single thing.

Conference Report. April, 1938, p. 30.

I was talking in one of the stakes of Zion to a bunch of careless Seventies, and I was trying to inject into them a little faith. Some fellow bawled out, "How do you get faith?" Well, it was such a sudden shock to me, I said, "I'll be blamed if I know." I told one of the greatest truths I have spoken for some time although somewhat crude.

Conference Report. October, 1922, p. 170.

And the Prophet Joseph Smith left with us this statement: "Where there are no gifts there is no faith."

Conference Report. October, 1930, p. 58.

And I will say right here, as far as God is concerned, and Jesus Christ, there is no disease that is incurable, if faith is exercised.

Conference Report. October, 1922, p. 171.

I remember a story of two elders wandering in the South without purse or scrip, and they came to a corn crib, and one of the elders said, "We will sleep there tonight," and he called that faith! It was, but it was a poor faith. Those boys wandered around and around and got lost, and traveled in a circle; and when darkness set in there was the corn crib, and the elder said, "There, I told you we would sleep in the corn crib." The Lord fulfilled his word, and it served him right. It is where he expected to sleep. "As your faith is, so shall it be unto you."

Conference Report. April, 1926, p. 61.

The Lord has taken care of me, and I have learned to trust him, as he is a good Master, and he is full of mercy, justice, kindness and love.

Conference Report. April, 1918, p. 133.

34

When you think of it for one moment it requires a great big belief to believe all that God does now reveal; "and we believe that He will yet reveal many great and important things pertaining to the kingdom of God." It is not very difficult for a Latter-day Saint to believe all that has been revealed. To me it is all true, but the great trouble I am having is to make it work.

Conference Report. April, 1915, p. 133.

After I had traveled for a year without purse or scrip and had tested God thoroughly, I found the Lord's word good. He never failed me.

Conference Report. April, 1921, p. 179.

I have got a pretty good brain, but it has not been big enough to handle my body; I have tried to direct and control my body, but it wouldn't obey. I have been administered to by some of the best men in this Church; no better men ever lived than the men who have administered to me, but I am sorry to say, and ashamed to say,

I did not have the faith to be healed. There is not a man in this Church who knows any better than I do that God the Father and Jesus Christ the Redeemer are the great physicians. I have unfaltering, unwavering faith in God the Father and in his Son Jesus Christ, but you cannot be healed without faith; you have got to have the faith. I have got the faith to heal others. I have seen some wonderful healings. Few men have seen more, unless they were better men. I have witnessed all kinds of diseases healed, but I could not get the faith. I failed. I just had enough faith to keep alive, that is all.

Conference Report. April, 1921, p. 180.

FAMILY

My family has been secondary in my work. I hope the brethren will be awfully careful what they say about families. I hope they will be very tender of men's feelings, when they talk about our children and about parents being responsible for their children—that their sins will rest upon them. God knows, I have got all I can carry without packing anyone else. . . .They are God's children. My children are God's children. God is just as much responsible for my children as I am.

Conference Report. April, 1921, p. 181.

Now I pray the Lord to bless you. You go right home now. I know where my trouble is, and I am trying to cure it. I am learning this lesson, that there is no use of my trying to govern a family until I govern myself.

Conference Report. April, 1913, p. 90.

I was born in this Church, and if there is any one thing

that I am proud of it is that I am a member of this Church. You Latter-day Saints know well how proud I am of my parentage. When I stop believing in my father and mother I will stop believing in the human family; for where they go I want to go.

Conference Report. April, 1905, p. 53.

The father almost needs the patience of Job to get a family together for morning prayer. That is pretty plain talk, but you seem to understand what I mean. I guess you have tried it.

Conference Report. April, 1913, p. 89.

I want eternal life. I want salvation, and I desire to breathe the same desire into my wife and children, so that they will want to partake of it, and be willing to make some sacrifice.

Conference Report. April, 1915, p. 135.

FELLOWSHIP

My brethren and sisters, I have this to say in conclusion: Even if you are in a hurry, stop and shake hands before going on, but do it right; have the spirit of God within you, and when you greet them say, "God bless you." I know a good old sister, who is working for her living; she would not let the Church support her, she is too proud. She is over 70 years old. She said to me that when an Apostle took her by the hand and said "God bless you" it was worth more to her than all the money they could give her. I remember Apostle Erastus Snow, and I will never forget him as long as I live on the earth. He stopped long enough to take me by the hand as a boy, after my father was dead, and said "God bless you."

Conference Report. April, 1899, p. 54.

I desire to call your attention to an incident that occured when I was laboring in the Southern States, in 1884. I went there in 1883. The year 1884 was a time of a sad experience in that mission. It was then that some of our Elders lost their lives by mob violence. It seemed that there was bitterness on all hands. We had but few friends. I was at the office in Chattanooga under Elder Roberts at the time. I picked up a Chattanooga Times one morning, and I was very much delighted to see in print these words, speaking of Elder John Morgan. It said, "To shake his hand was to be his friend." I have never forgotten it. When you shook John Morgan's hand and he looked into your face you always knew that you were his friend. John Morgan understood that principle. Some of our people are becoming careless in the shaking of hands. I have shaken hands with some men, when I would just as soon have put my hand into a bucket of ice water as to shake hands with them. They may have been friendly, but I have no means of telling. Great sermons have been preached in this Church by the simple shaking of hands; and you who have been in holy places, you who have been in the holy temple, know what it means to shake hands.

Conference Report. April, 1899, p. 53.

GENEALOGY

I am very proud of my parentage. I do not think any one appreciates their parentage more than I do. But, I want to say to the Latter-day Saints, pride in parentage won't save you.

Conference Report. April, 1913, p. 85.

GOALS

I do not know just where I am going, but I know mighty well I am on my way.

Conference Report. April, 1911, p. 69.

I claim that it is my right to become rich and to surround myself with the riches of the world, inasmuch as I use it for the good of the children of men. But I have no further ambition in that direction, unless I am specially called by those appointed to labor in the Church. I have, however, an ambition to be saved in the kingdom of my Father. I desire to understand the Gospel, the plan of life and salvation, and if there is any greater ambition that can be given unto the children of men, I pray you to point out the pathway.

Conference Report. October, 1898, p. 17.

I am going to ask you a few questions and then conclude my remarks. I wonder if we Seventies know what we want? I know my father preached once, "that to want a thing and you can't get it is hell." Some people have never been able to find out what they want. I have learned that when my family want anything they seem to want it mighty bad, and I never have much peace until I get it for them.

Conference Report. April, 1915, p. 134.

I know what I want, and I begin to find out what it will cost.

Conference Report. April, 1915, p. 135.

GOLDEN RULE

I think of what Elbert Hubbard said. It struck me rather strangely the other day. He said: "If you are going to reform the world you had better begin with yourself, and there will be one rogue less in the world." Of course I did not want to apply that to myself, but I would not object to applying it to you.

Conference Report. October, 1921, p. 83.

Bishop John B. Maiben gives an interesting link in the historic chain at the time of the famine. "Some individuals who had flour sold it at $25 to $30 a 100 pounds. Not so with Heber, for at no time did he charge more than $6 a 100 pounds, then the standard tithing-office price. He distributed in various amounts, from five to fifty pounds to the poor, amounting to about 30,000 pounds. His acts of generosity, mercy and charity, during this time of sore distress, are worthy of the man. He kept an open house and fed from twenty-five to one hundred poor people at the tables daily, with bread, flour and other necessities that were worth their weight in gold."

Conference Report. April, 1928, p. 78.

If you honor your wife and speak well of her, other people will do so. If you do not honor your children and you have a hired girl in the house and you do not treat them kindly, the girl herself will treat your own children unkindly.

Conference Report. October, 1900, p. 54.

GRATITUDE

Did you ever make a Christmas present to a child, and when they got it they were disappointed, and your Christmas was ruined, and you were made to feel almost broken-hearted, when you had affectionately expended every dollar you had, and because other people's children had presents much better, the whole day was spoiled to them and to you, too? Ingratitude is a sin in the sight of God.

Conference Report. April, 1913, p. 87.

HAPPINESS

In standing before the Latter-day Saints this afternoon, I desire to say those things that are timely, and to speak under the influence of the Holy Spirit. Notwithstanding the seriousness of the occasion, having met as a part of the great Annual Conference, we need not pull long faces and put on an air of self righteousness, thinking it indicates faith and is more pleasing to the Lord. The Lord has said, "Cease from your light speeches, and excess of laughter," but He surely is pleased with pleasant countenances and a happy people, although wit and humor, may be out of place in houses of worship. I read somewhere the following: "Many persons who never had a bright idea in their heads, or a generous sentiment in their hearts, assuming an air of owlish wisdom, affect to disdain wit and humor, having never heard of the great truth enunciated by Charles Lamb: 'A laugh is worth a hundred groans in any market.' The idea is propagated that mutual dryness is indicative of wisdom." I realize that my reputation for wisdom has been greatly injured by repeating jokes in my public utterances, and that, because of my calling in the ministry, I should, in the estimation of some people be as solemn as an owl.

Conference Report. April, 1906, p. 74.

Men are that they might have joy. Happiness is the object and design of our creation and will be to the end of our existence if we pursue the path that leads to it. This path is virtue, uprightness, faithfulness, holiness. To keep God's commandments we must know them. To know them we must read the scriptures and repent and be in tune with the Holy Spirit and he will lead us into all truth and show us things to come. I promise you that you shall hear a voice behind you saying, this is the way, walk ye in it.

Conference Report. October, 1926, pp. 130-131.

HEALTH

When I was in California I was very low spirited and broken down in body; and I tried to die, but I made a miserable failure of it.

Conference Report. October, 1910, p. 34.

I know I have spent a good deal of time, brethren in trying to live. About Christmas, 1923, I thought I was dying. I had a hemorrhage of the lungs, and I bled quantities of blood. I thought I hardly had a pint left in me. I sent for my wife and handed her the keys to my safety box and said: "Here is the key to my safety box; there is nothing in it. God bless you." I then sent for a great specialist to examine me and see what was the matter. He examined me and said, "How old are you?" I said, "I am seventy years old." "Well," he said, "I thought you were forty-seven." I replied, "If that is the way you look at it, I am going to get out of here," and I did.

Conference Report. April, 1925, p. 121.

He [B. H. Roberts] was to be trusted. I was sick and he ministered to me and was so kind and patient. I had boils—called carbuncles, if you know what a carbuncle is. I don't know what kind of boils Job had, but if he had carbuncles I am in full sympathy for him.

Conference Report. October, 1933, p. 42.

I feel happy, just as happy as a man can feel with the rheumatism.

Conference Report. October, 1906, p. 117.

I feel a good deal like the story I read the other day. "Some fellow was sitting on the pier that reached out into the ocean—and he fell in, and he holloed, "Help! help! I can't swim." And an old fellow was sitting on the pier fishing, and he said: "Neither can I, but I wouldn't brag about it." I don't want to brag about sickness, because it is a kind of a disgrace to get sick in this Church, and not have faith to be healed.

Conference Report. October, 1922, p. 170.

I am very glad that I am not so old as I feel.

Conference Report. April, 1938, p. 29.

HOLY GHOST

I remember when I was presiding over the Southern States mission: for two years of that time I brought home two emigrations a year, and when I went to the President's office to report, that great Prophet, the President of the Church, Wilford Woodruff, who was interested in me, said: "Brother Kimball, sit down a minute." We had only a few minutes—it didn't take five minutes. He told me more than once: "Now, Brother Kimball, I have had visions, I have had revelations, I have seen angels, but the greatest of all is that still small voice."

Conference Report. April, 1924, p. 70.

When I thought I had the Spirit of the Lord, some of the people did not think so. So that you can never tell; and if you say there is such a man living upon the earth, however inspired he may be, or however good a man he may be, who can please and satisfy all people, I question whether that man ever lived. I know mighty well I am not one of them.

Conference Report. April, 1924, p. 69.

So that sometimes, and very often, the servants of God speak by the Spirit of God, but some of the people haven't got the same spirit, and do not believe the servants of God. Now, brethren, I want to express to you this thought, that it is just as necessary for you Latter-day Saints to have the Spirit of God as it is for the apostles and seventies and the presidents of stakes and the bishops, for when you speak, or when the servants of

God speak under the influence of the Holy Spirit, it is the word of God to the Latter-day Saints.

Conference Report. October, 1918, p. 30.

Brethren and sisters, I have a conviction burning within me, sometimes like a living fire. There are a lot of things I do not know, but I know some things. I have paid the price. I have eaten the bread of adversity. I have drunk the water of affliction, and I have found God. I have told you that before. I have found God, and he has answered my prayers. I have heard that still small Voice—we call it a Voice—spoken to me not infrequently and whenever I followed it I was right. So that I can say with you that I am blessed in all my ways, because the Father gives to me of his Holy Spirit to guide and direct me in every situation, if I am humble and contrite in spirit and in truth.

Conference Report. October, 1924, p. 71.

I grant you that men holding authority have a right to reprove sharply, but they must be sure that they are moved upon by the Holy Ghost.

Conference Report. April, 1907, p. 81.

Experience teaches me that when I have been angry, I am quite sure I did not have the Holy Ghost, and I was not in any proper condition to administer reproof. It took me quite a long while to learn that. When I became excited, fanatical, and over-zealous, I mistakenly thought it was the Spirit of the Lord, but have learned better, as the Holy Ghost does not operate that way. My testimony is that the internal fruits of the Holy Ghost are joy, peace, patience, long suffering, and kindness.

Conference Report. April, 1907, p. 81.

HONESTY

What can God do for a man who is not honest? You may baptize him every fifteen minutes, but if he does not repent, he will come up out of the water just as dishonest as ever. What can God do for a liar who refuses to repent? Can the Lord save him? He can't claim salvation. Baptising him in water will not settle the trouble, unless you keep him under.

Conference Report. April, 1909, p. 37.

This call has come somewhat unexpected, although I try in my labors in the ministry to always think about something and then try to tell it. Now, if there is any one thing that I am normal in, it is frankness. Whenever the time comes, in my ministerial labors, that I cannot be frank and honest with the people I will feel that my usefulness has come to an end.

Conference Report. April, 1913, p. 84.

JOURNAL

I never wrote a book in my life and never will, but I have written thousands of things and pigeon-holed them and never read them to anyone else but myself. I want to advise this people, if the Lord ever does give you an inspiration, for heaven's sake write it down and remember it. If Joseph Smith the prophet had not done that, you would never have had some things contained in the Doctrine and Covenants.

Conference Report. April, 1927, pp. 52-53.

Now, I want to say to you that a while back I was sick, two or three weeks, with what they call the "flu." I inherited that disease; I get it every little while. While I was there I wondered if I had exaggerated my experience in the South, so I hunted up my diaries which I had not read for forty years, and I discovered that I told the truth. The record is as correct as the record of the Bible, and I was astonished how God blessed me and how I enjoyed his spirit and the manifestations and testimonies that were given to me.

Conference Report. April, 1927, p. 52.

When I find a good idea—which is not very often, for very few of us do—I write it down. When you get an idea, write it down. That is what the Prophet Joseph tried to teach this people. When the Lord gives you a sudden idea, write it down, and then watch it; and if it comes from God, through his Spirit, it is inspiration; and when it comes true, that is revelation.

Conference Report. April, 1926, p. 59.

JUDGMENT

Now, brethren, you can judge yourselves. Do not bother about me. Be concerned about yourselves, and I will get along the best way I can. If I do not make it, there is no reason why you should not; and if I can make it, anybody can make it. That is my personal idea. I do not know whether that is an encouragement to you or not.

Conference Report. April, 1926, p. 47.

I may not stand blameless before God at the last day,

but I am not afraid to meet my God and be judged by the Lord as to my desires, efforts and works. I understand the gospel of Jesus Christ well enough to know that God is perfect and deals out justice and mercy to his children; Jesus is the door to the sheep-fold, and with all my many imperfections and weaknesses, if I am invited by the Master to come in at the door, all men who try to block my way will get run over and pushed aside.

Conference Report. April, 1918, p. 133.

JUSTICE

I am not going to announce any blood and thunder doctrine to you today. I have not been radical for four long months, not since I had appendicitis. I came very nearly being operated upon. I thought I was going to die for a few hours. People said to me, "Why, brother Kimball, you needn't be afraid, you'll get justice." "Well," I said, "that is what I am afraid of."

Conference Report. October, 1905, p. 81.

LOVE

Now, brethren, let us repent, if we have got any bitterness in our hearts toward each other, let us be generous, and forgiving. No man has any influence or power for good when angry.

Conference Report. April, 1909, p. 38.

The great test was: "By this shall all men know that ye are my disciples, if ye have love one to another."

If you have not love for one another you have not the spirit of the gospel.

Conference Report. October, 1917, pp. 136-137.

We should learn to love and honor each other. We should have the spirit of God burning within our hearts. You can make more converts in this way than by any other means.

Conference Report. April, 1899, p. 54.

MARRIAGE

I ask the Latter-day Saint husbands if you have wives that look at everything just like you do? I would not give a snap of my finger for a woman that did not fight for her rights. I am thankful that my wife happens to be one of that kind; she has her own personality, her own individuality and we don't always see things just alike.

Conference Report. April, 1913, p. 89.

We do not want any Seventies that are run by their wives either. I do not blame the wives for running their husbands, because I think we have Seventies that their wives ought to run. I hear it almost every day (I do not want you to think it is at home either) "What a lovely husband that man is. If I only had a husband like that I would be happy." I ask what kind of a husband he is. "Well, he shakes the quilts, he puts the carpets down, he helps wash the dishes, he helps dress the children," etc. Well if it takes all that to make a good man, you cannot count me in among them. I would rather go on a mission, and I would rather stay and die with my neck in the collar. I think it is honorable to do these things when you are at home, but if I have to do them, I want to stay at home but a very little while. I do not believe that God gave a man the Holy Melchisedek Priesthood and ordained him a Seventy in the Church of Jesus Christ, to be tagging after one little woman and spending his whole life in that way. That is what I want to say to you Seventies; I have said it and I don't propose to take it back.

Conference Report. October, 1899, pp. 54-55.

I was with an apostle on a trip in the south, and we found a bishop without any people. He wept, and came to the apostle to know what to do. "Well you will have to stay here until some people come to you." All the people he had was his wife, and anybody that can preside over his wife, I take my hat off to him.

Conference Report. April, 1924, p. 70.

49

MATERIALISM

It is not a difficult thing to live in a log hut if you have never had anything better, but it is a difficult thing to drop to a log house when you have been living in a castle.

Conference Report. April, 1898, p. 43.

Today, at the dawn of the twentieth century, we, as Latter-day Saints, are in sore need of a vision of the future which will uplift us above and beyond the petty, sordid interests of the moment, viz: That money devil, intemperance, and immorality, are some of the evils which are lying right across the highway of our future. It is riches, automobiles, oriental rugs, fashion, social functions, class distinction, and other worldly things that appeal to our covetousness more than just doing right, for they are advertised better and have a stronger appeal to our sordid natures.

Conference Report. April, 1934, p. 34.

The prodigal dollar seems to be swallowing all that is great and noble with some of the new and rising generation.

Conference Report. April, 1927, p. 56.

50

One good mother stated that her son wrote her and said, "I have only $3, and if you do not send me some money I will be licking the paste off the signboards." And the mother came to me somewhat disturbed and said: "Brother Kimball, what shall I do?" I said, "Let him lick paste for a while; he will find the Lord, but he never will with a pocket full of money."

Conference Report. April, 1926, p. 60.

MEDIA

I guess there is a reporter here isn't there? I am always afraid of those "blooming reporters;" they always get things down as I say it, but it don't sound well. It sounds all right when I deliver it, but it doesn't read well in print.

Conference Report. October, 1922, p. 170.

My brethren and sisters, in a few words I desire to say to you that I think the things of the world are better advertised than the things of God. When I hear those beautiful voices over the radio, advertising the things of the world, I am wonderstruck. If there is anything under heaven they do not advertise, and give it away at a dollar a week, I do not know what it is. By the time they get through with us—the "Lucky Strike" puts over their wonderful music—no wonder smokers' mouths water after hearing it.

Conference Report. October, 1931, p. 57.

MEETINGS

The people had not seen an Apostle for twenty years, and it was Sunday, a fast day. Meetings were begun in the morning and they kept them up all day, and we were fasting. I was pretty nearly dead at four o'clock. After four o'clock Brother Lyman said, "Now, Brother Kimball, get up and tell them about the *Era*." He had done a good deal of talking himself about the *Era*. During that trip I think we got four hundred subscribers—$800.00. I wrote out all receipts. It was in September. Brother Lyman at this meeting told me to get up, so I did, and I said: "All you men that will take the *Era* if we will let you go home, raise your right hand." There was not a single man who did not raise his hand and subscribed and paid $2.00 for the *Era*. Brother Lyman said: "That is the brightest thing you ever did." I do not claim that was inspiration; it was good psychology. Really they paid $2.00 to get out.

Conference Report. April, 1932, p. 78.

I am about through. You are the best outstanding crowd I ever talked to in my life. You know how it is; we get people to talk to inside, and lock them in, so they can't get out! I remember being up north. I said, "All you people that want to go, go;" and they nearly all went, and I didn't blame them.

Conference Report. October, 1922, p. 173.

MISSIONARY

We are almost immune to missionary work....

Conference Report. April, 1915, p. 133.

I am now going to ask you a few questions: "Do you know of anything in all this beautiful world that is more important than human life?" You don't, do you? I will ask the same question in another way: "Do you know of anything in all this great universe that is dearer to the Father than a human soul?" You don't do you? Of course you don't, as the Lord said in the Doctrine and Covenants, "And if it so be that you should labor all your days in crying repentance unto this people, and bring save it be one soul unto me, how great will be your joy with him in the kingdom of my Father."

Conference Report. April, 1918, p. 133.

The first time I ever saw Elder Roberts was either in Cincinnati or St. Louis. He had been chosen as president of the Southern States Mission to succeed John Morgan. I left for Chattanooga, Tennessee, with twenty-seven elders assigned to the Southern States. There were all kinds of elders in the company—farmers, cowboys, few educated—a pretty hard looking crowd, and I was one of that kind. The elders preached, and talked, and sang, and advertised loudly their calling as preachers. I kept still for once in my life; I hardly opened my mouth . I saw a gentleman get on the train. I can visualize that man now. I didn't know who he was. He knew we were a band of Mormon elders. The elders soon commenced a discussion and argument with the stranger, and before he got through they were in grave doubt about their message of salvation. He gave them a training that they never forgot. That man proved to be President B. H. Roberts.

Conference Report. October, 1933, pp. 42-43.

When I was in the mission field, I said to the Elders: Whenever you are moved upon by the Spirit of God, and the spirit of testimony, you are to testify that Joseph Smith is a Prophet of God, and I promise you it will make you all the trouble you can bear.

Conference Report. April, 1908, p. 115.

I know of no better way to make this clear to you than to relate an incident that happened in my missionary experience, at the time I was appointed to preside over the Southern States mission. I succeeded Elder William Spry. There was only a few days notice given me. The brethren failed to inquire regarding my financial condition, my wife and children, my physical condition, or whether my teeth were all right, etc.; they just appointed me without asking me any questions, and I had faith enough to go. The itinerary was made out by Elder Spry to visit those conferences which occurred only once a year, as the mission covered eleven states. We had the means to go through that mission only once a year. In fact, when Elder Spry turned the mission over to me he handed me thirty-five dollars. I said: "Is that all you've got?"

"Yes."

"How do you get your money?"

"Why, we go to the Lord and ask him."
"Well," I said, "I don't think he is very liberal."

Conference Report. October, 1931, pp. 55-56.

During my labors in Chattanooga with Brother Roberts, as it was in the early history of that city, I was thoroughly poisoned with malaria. I was drunken, but not with strong drink, but with malaria. I was as yellow as a parchment. As I went along the streets one day in Chattanooga, a stranger met me. He happened to be a physician. He said, "Young man, I don't know who you are, but if you don't do something for yourself you will die." "Well," I said, "I will not, as I am a 'Mormon,' you can't kill them." When Brother Morgan came down and relieved Brother Roberts, I was still in the office, looking worse than ever. Brother Morgan looked me over carefully. He said, "Brother Kimball, you better go home. The mission is very hard run for money. It will only cost twenty-four dollars to send you home alive, but it will cost three hundred to send you home dead." It was a matter of business in that office; they had no money. I think maybe that was all I was worth. "No," I said, "Brother Morgan, I don't want to go home. I believe I was called on this mission by revelation; at least they told me so in my blessing. Now God has been good to me and he has been faithful and true, and I want to test him out, and if he can't take care of me, when I have been as faithful and true as I have, and made the sacrifices I have, then he is not the God of my fathers." So Brother Morgan let me stay, and I filled my mission. I have my release. It is the only release I have ever had, and I prize it very much.

Conference Report. April, 1921, p. 179.

I said to my companion, who was from the Brigham

Young Academy, "Let us go up into the woods and see if we can sing," (I couldn't carry a tune, I never tried to sing in the Academy), "and let us go up and learn to pray." We did not have any audience, only those great big trees. And I said "Let us learn to preach." I would advise young elders to do that before they start out and not practice so much on the people; we practiced on the trees.

Conference Report. October, 1925, p. 158.

At one time I was up in the Blue Ridge mountains of Virginia, in the winter, with a straw hat and a duster on. It was not very suitable; it was not very warm. We could not wear overcoats; could not carry them in that country. All we carried was an umbrella. We never were at a loss to know what to do, my companion and I when we had the spirit of our calling. We heard that voice—not very often, not as often as we should have done, but we heard it—behind us saying, "This is the way, walk ye in it, when ye turn to the right and when ye turn to the left." I stand before you as a witness for God that he never forsook us. I walked—and I am a very poor walker; I am not built for it—hundreds and hundreds of miles, and I never lay outdoors but twice, though I want to confess to you I hustled. There is nothing I dreaded worse than lying outside on the ground. I prayed, and my companion prayed, and then we got up and moved on. I guess we would have starved to death if we had kept praying and not hustled; the Lord doesn't help people who do not hustle and move, after they pray, and do their duty.

Conference Report. April, 1926, p. 59.

I don't think we need spend very much time troubling over our enemies, and I don't believe in sticking pins in them. Take no more notice of them than you would of a fice dog. One time, in the south, it was my companion's turn to ask for entertainment, and he stood on a platform nearly as high as my head, and knocked on the door; just then one of those little fice dogs bounded out the doorway, ran right between my companion's legs and landed on top of my head. That is the only time I ever was frightened by a fice dog, and I never have been frightened since.

Conference Report. October, 1905, p. 82.

56

After you have been ordained a seventy, by proper authority, if the time never comes in your life that you desire to go on a mission, and that you make no effort to go, it shall be evidence to you that you are not a witness for God, that the spirit of your calling has not yet come to you. Now, I take it for granted it won't come very often to some of us, but it ought to come in every man's life in this Church—that he has that hunger, that desire, and makes the effort to be a witness for God and preach the gospel.

Conference Report. April, 1911, p. 71.

An incident happened in the Southern States mission, which I will relate. It transpired in the days of President John Morgan, and occurred at a time when the State of Tennessee passed a law that any man who advocated or preached polygamy was to be arrested and punished. Enemies to the Elders entrapped the brethren into a discussion on this most unpopular subject, and the Elders defended the principle from a Biblical standpoint. A complaint was filed, and the Elders were arrested. They were short of room inside the jail, so the brethren, two in number, were confined in two steel cages on the outside, near to each other. The imprisoned servants of the Lord were not orators or singers. The people far and near, hearing of Mormon Elders being under arrest, gathered to see these peculiar individuals. The brethren sang hymns and testified of the truth of the Gospel, etc. It is claimed they had congregations of 300, and I have been told that the people had never heard such wonderful preaching and singing. The Elders almost regretted receiving their freedom. So I am almost inclined to advocate putting our Elders in jail once in a while, when they are unable to get a hearing in any other way.

Conference Report. April, 1906, p. 75.

I will go on a mission if called. I am not just talking either, God knows it, and I know it. I would go if I were brought back in a casket, and I do not know but I would be tickled to death to have it come that way.

Conference Report. October, 1925, p. 159.

MORMONS

I don't stand with bated breath for fear this Church will be destroyed. This is the work of God; this is the Church of Jesus Christ. There are not devils enough to destroy it, and it can't be destroyed by men. If it could have been destroyed, some who claim to be members in the Church would have destroyed it years ago.

Conference Report. October, 1904, p. 57.

My temperament is such that I cannot say anything inspiring, or bubble with enthusiasm, and be clear, happy, or joyous, if I have to wear a restraining collar and cater to popular sentiments. I would like my preaching to have color, thrill, feel homelike, and revive old memories, and myself feel free as a colt in a pasture. Now, if I can't feel that way among the Latter-day Saints, where on earth can I go that I will feel free?

Conference Report. October, 1912, p. 26.

I always say, God save the people, for if it were not for people, we would not need this great Church.

Conference Report. April, 1924, p. 70.

I know a good deal more about this Church than the man did, one of those strangers that come in our midst, who went on a hill here recently and stood in an ant bed, and when the ants commenced to bite he commenced to curse the "Mormons." I suppose he thought they were "Mormon" ants, and he held us responsible for them.

Conference Report. October, 1904, p. 57.

OBEDIENCE

To keep God's commandments we must know them. To know them we must read the scriptures and repent and be in tune with the Holy Spirit and he will lead us into all truth and show us things to come.

Conference Report. October, 1937, p. 33.

I am not sure if we will be prepared to receive all or not. Joseph Smith said the Lord had revealed things to him which if he had repeated to the people they would have taken his life. It is a good thing he didn't; we have more truths and doctrine than we now live up to.

Conference Report. April, 1909, p. 37.

I feel to bless the people. I feel that you are being blessed and that you will continue to be blessed as long as you keep the commandments of God. When you cease keeping the commandments of God then the judgments of God will commence at the house of the Lord, and I pray that that may be averted. I pray that we may not pass through the experience that the people had in Kirtland because they transgressed the laws of God.

Conference Report. April, 1898, pp. 44-45.

I am sure, from the experience I have had in the Church, that the Lord can do very little for a man who persists in being dishonest and untruthful; and, of course, it goes without saying that no man or woman in the Church of Jesus Christ can be immoral and have the Spirit of God to be with him.

Conference Report. October, 1921, p. 83.

59

PATRIOTISM

I don't know that I can tell you how I feel during this conference, any better than to tell you how I felt when I was down to the Chicamaugua Park, when they were mobilizing soldiers for the war. They mobilized forty thousand soldiers at that place, and one day I saw there nine thousand soldiers under dress parade, and I heard the martial music, and I saw them pass under the great flag of the United States, and every one of them doffed his hat when he came to the flag. My blood coursed rapidly through my veins, and I felt as if I was eight or ten feet tall, and that I would like to go to the war and see how it felt. I don't know how long the feeling would have lasted, but I never felt better in my life. I never felt more inspired with that kind of inspiration and loyalty to the United States than I did on that one occasion. It has been the occasion of my life, and I learned that I was patriotic, that I was loyal, that the blood of the revolutionary fathers coursed through my veins, and I was mighty glad to find out. I felt just the same way during this conference, and I wouldn't be afraid of all the world, all the devils in hell, if I could always have the same spirit of inspiration that has actuated me during this conference.

Conference Report. October, 1900, p. 53.

PERSECUTION

I want to ask in all soberness, if you think this Gospel that has been revealed by the Lord through the Prophet Joseph Smith can be advocated and preached among the children of men without serious consequences? I tell you if our Elders go out and advocate the truth of this work, it will bring upon them persecution, and whippings. It may not be the better element who will do that, they never have whipped our Elders, it has generally been the same class as those who are killing the negroes in the South; but the people winked at it. I was almost a witness to the killing of our Elders in Tennessee, on Cane Creek, and I know something about the spirit of mobocracy.

Conference Report. April, 1906, pp. 75-76.

PERSPECTIVE

I have tried to be generous in my sentiments, and be on the right side; I have tried to be tolerant, not intolerant, I have tried to respect men's opinions, and I have discovered that we do not always see things alike. We may as far as the gospel is concerned, but we are a long way from it in other things. In temporal things we do not sufficiently respect each other's opinions.

Conference Report. April, 1909, pp. 37-38.

I desire to say to you that my life is being crystallized into a very few things that are important to me. The great hope that I have is to be saved in the kingdom of God.

Conference Report. October, 1929, p. 57.

The Lord is very patient with His people, with His children. I often think of the time when I was in the South, laboring as an elder in Virginia. The president of the conference in which I was appointed was called into Colorado to continue teaching the people. He shed tears, because he wanted to stay in the Southern States mission, and "bind up the law and seal up the testimony;" he wanted to condemn all the people and close up the mission so the end would come. That was in 1883. We have had a great many elders who would have closed our missionary labors, as far as the world was concerned, but the Lord is not so short sighted and impatient. He has all eternity, and He proposes to save His children "excepting the sons of perdition."

Conference Report. October, 1910, p. 32.

I look over my past labors in the ministry, and I discover there were some things that I didn't know.

Conference Report. April, 1908, p. 115.

We all have different viewpoints, and perhaps there is not one man in Israel that will look at a thing in just the same way, from just the same view point I look at it. If I do look at it from a different view point from you, I want to ask the question, Am I wrong? And I answer, 'Not unless I preach false doctrine.

Conference Report. April, 1913, p. 86.

POLITICS

I feel to say, "God save the people, not kings, but the people." If I had written that poetry, I would have said, "God save the people"—and to _____ with the kings, but as I didn't write it, will refrain from saying it.

Conference Report. April, 1918, p. 133.

For the past month or so, I have been reading political platforms, and promises, and pledges enough to last the people of these United States for a thousand years, if they are carried out. I don't believe in making many promises or pledges, but when you do make them, and issue a platform, I say try and live up to it.

Conference Report. October, 1912, p. 26.

In the midst of an election in Denver, a little girl sat in a church with her suffragette mother, listening to a minister who was preaching with much earnestness and emphatic gestures. When he had finished the little girl turned to her mother and asked: "Mother, was he for or against God?"

Conference Report. October, 1912, p. 27.

I want to tell you that while I am a member of the Church of Jesus Christ of Latter-day Saints, I have my franchise, and my citizenship, and I have my vote, and I have a right to cast it. And if every single man or woman that is entitled to their franchise, instead of going and howling after the trouble is over, would shake themselves and realize that they are members of this great nation and great State, and go to their primaries and cast their ballot, I tell you mighty few dishonest men would find their way into our State and into the offices. But it is your fault, because we do not do our duty as American citizens.

Conference Report. October, 1900, p. 54.

PRAYER

It was during that period of time that I found God; as my father said: God answered my prayers, and isn't that a pretty good evidence that God lives?

Conference Report. October, 1930, p. 58.

I feel a good deal, I think, like my father did one time when he was praying. You know he was rather peculiar, and prayed in his own way. He was praying about someone, and he stopped in his prayer and laughed very heartily, and then said, "O Lord, forgive me, it makes me laugh to pray about some men."

Conference Report. October, 1905, p. 81.

Prayer can be made in a simple, humble manner, without using a multitude of words.

Conference Report. April, 1913, p. 88.

Father had men working for him a good many years, and he had one he called Col. Smith. It was in the days of hardships and poverty, and men had great difficulty. They employed a great many people, the brethren did, that was a part of their religion. He employed the colonel, who had been a soldier in Great Britain, and on one occasion he went to father for a pair of shoes, and I guess father felt pretty cross, and answered him a little abruptly, perhaps. So the Colonel went home feeling badly, and when he prayed that night, he made a complaint to God against father, saying that "Thy servant Heber" was not treating him right. When he came past that little place on Gordon Avenue, next morning, father came out and said, "Robert, what did you complain against me for? You come in and get your shoes, and don't do it again!" Now, how did he know that Col. Robert Smith, who lived away down in the Nineteenth ward, had filed a complaint against him? Don't you think that we can get on friendly terms with God? Not on familiar terms, but friendly terms.

Conference Report. April, 1913, p. 90.

There is divine wisdom in praying always and avoiding the very appearance of evil.

Conference Report. October, 1937, p. 33.

When I was a boy, my father did most of the praying in the home, and when I got to manhood I did not know how to pray; I did not know just how or what to pray for. In fact, I did not know very much about the Lord, because my father died when I was fifteen years old, but I can remember how he prayed, and I have been sorry, many times, that I can't pray like my father did, for he seemed on those occasions to be in personal communication with God. There seemed to be a friendliness between my father and God, and when you heard him pray you would actually think the Lord was right there, and that father was talking to Him. Can you pray that way? Are you on such friendly terms with the Lord? I don't mean that we should get too friendly and take advantage of it, like children with parents, but that we should manifest reverence and love for the Lord, ask only for what we need, and not for what we want.

Conference Report. April, 1913, p. 86.

PRIESTHOOD

Why is it that we are different from other men in the world? It is not because we have greater knowledge and information, but because we hold the Priesthood.

Conference Report. April, 1906, p. 19.

Why is it that you fathers and mothers permit your 18-year-old boys to go to South Africa, Australia, Germany, or other nations of the earth, notwithstanding you are afraid to trust them out in this city after dark? It is because they hold the Priesthood. Our beardless boys are able to defend the Church of Jesus Christ, and preach the Gospel. They hold divine authority. . . . There is no great number of men in this Church so carefully looked after, and their lives so well preserved, as are the Elders who preach the Gospel in the world.

Conference Report. April, 1906, p. 19.

PROGRESSION

I am not converted to the theory of the mother that taught her child "to hang her clothes on a hickory limb and not go near the water," for we must be reaching, climbing, towering and trying to prepare ourselves for the great events of life. There is always some chance to be taken and it is expected that mistakes will be made and that "we will change our opinions and correct our mistakes.

Conference Report. October, 1901, p. 56.

One of our Bishops in early days was accustomed to floating logs down the Mississippi River. Occasionally one would break loose and find its way into a whirlpool, and it would go round and round until it was wasted away. The log was travelling all the time but was left behind and made no progress.

Conference Report. October, 1901, p. 56.

We have had the Holy Ghost conferred upon us for many years. I was baptized and received the laying on of hands when eight years old. I have not made my election sure. I have not attained to that great desire as yet. Are we going to be satisfied and cease to hunger and thirst after righteousness, and the moment we meet with adversity and trouble, lay down and cease our progression and advancement? I have seen new colonies of the Saints built up in some of our little settlements almost like magic. They reached a certain place with their improvements and like the Arkansas traveler became satisfied and made no further improvements. I am sometimes fearful that many of our people "climb their little hill:" and then go down again. Young people get married, and oftentimes reach a place where all climbing, towering and reaching out after knowledge ceases and they merely eke out an existence. To see young men with such grand opportunities and prospects stop and wait for something to come to them is most deplorable. I ask you, to consider the changes, advancement and improvement your foreign missionary Elders undergo after a brief mission of two years. Their very being is changed, but not the frequency with which they cease progression and fall back to old habits, and become "mentally lazy."

Conference Report. October, 1901, p. 57.

I do not expect to become a god, right away. No, it will take a long time; I am too ignorant. When I stand before my Maker, in the other world, I will be like some of those poor Elders who have been laboring in missions, I will speak with a stammering tongue, and God will look upon me, no doubt, as a child, mediocre in intelligence compared with those who have preceded me.

Conference Report. April, 1907, p. 82.

67

PROPHECY

I am going to read you something that was said three years after I was born. That is a very long time ago. It seems to me like a hundred years. A prophet of God said it, and it is coming true every day, but it has taken a long time to fulfil the prophecy. In the year 1856—Heber C. Kimball said: "We think we are secure here in the chambers of the everlasting hills, but I say to you, the time is coming when we will be mixed up in these now peaceful valleys to that extent that it will be difficult to tell the face of a Saint from the face of an enemy of the people of God." Can't you see its fulfilment?

Conference Report. April, 1923, p. 127.

I think of my father—our father, the father of a great race of people—he prophecied once somewhere on these temple grounds, when the people were in poverty, when they were almost disheartened, and things looked so dark and dreary before them. Heber C. Kimball prophecied that goods would be sold as cheaply in Salt Lake City as in New York. After he sat down, he said to Brigham Young, "Well, Brother Brigham, I have done it now."

Brother Brigham said, "Never mind, Heber; let it go."

They did not, either one of them, believe it. (Laughter)

After the meeting adjourned, Apostle Charles C. Rich, I am told, went up to Heber C. Kimball, and he said, "Heber, I don't believe a word you said."

Heber said: "Neither do I." (Laughter) But he rounded it out: "But God hath spoken."

It was not Heber at all; it was God who spoke through Heber as a prophet. A short time after, the prophecy was literally fulfilled.

Conference Report. October, 1918, p. 30.

I have been told that I should prophesy. I want to say to you Latter-day Saints that to be a prophet of God all fear and all doubt have to leave your mind, and you then open your mouth and God gives you the words. But I have become so fearful about things I would be afraid to let it loose. I want to tell you there are a lot of us in the same fix. We are afraid of what people will think and are doubtful about its fulfilment.

Conference Report. October, 1932, p. 20.

It is related that during the famine, a brother, sorely in need of bread, came to President Kimball for counsel as to how to procure it. "Go and marry a wife," was Heber's terse reply, after feeding the brother. The man thought Brother Kimball must be out of his mind, but when he thought of his prophetic character, he resolved to obey counsel. He wondered where such a woman was and, thinking of a widow with several children, he got busy and proposed. As widows generally do, she accepted him. In that widow's house was laid up a six months' store of provisions. She surely grub-staked him. Meeting Brother Kimball soon after, the prosperous man of a family said: "Well, Brother Heber, I followed your advice." "Yes," said the man of God, "and you found bread."

Conference Report. April, 1928, p. 78.

I believe Joseph Smith is one of the greatest prophets that has ever lived. I believe in his prophecies and revelations. While I may be among the number that would like to rush things on a little, to see how they are coming out, in Jackson County and all that, I am sure that all will be literally fulfilled in the due time of the Lord.

Conference Report. April, 1930, p. 61.

If you prophesy do you stop to think about it, and wonder how the people will receive it? I take the position that there is no man living that was inspired of God, and prophesied in the name of the Lord, who took time to think about it; inspiration does not come that way.

Conference Report. April, 1911, p. 68.

PROPHETS

I have been acquainted with all the Prophets of God from the days of President Brigham Young down. They have been kind to me in my childhood and in my manhood. It does not matter much to me where the place is that they have gone to, but I want to tell you they are good enough company for me, and I do not want to go with any others, because I would be lonesome.

Conference Report. April, 1905, p. 55.

At family prayers, just a little while before his [Heber C. Kimball's] death, he remarked that the Angel Moroni had visited him the night before and had informed him that his work on this earth was finished and he would soon be taken.

He died the morning of June 22, 1868.

Conference Report. April, 1928, p. 80.

If any man can prove to me that Joseph Smith is not a prophet of God, he has taken everything; he has burned every bridge behind me. I never saw the Prophet, but I have heard my father often talk about him and I have read his revelations and his prophecies, as a witness for God, and I know they are true. He is a prophet of God.

Conference Report. October, 1926, pp. 131-132.

I have read about the Prophet Joseph Smith. I have the story of the Prophet, and it is a wonderful story for a boy to tell. About those two personages that came to him, also John the Baptist, Peter, James and John. To me it is very wonderful. Do you believe it? If that is not true, Joseph Smith was the biggest fraud that ever came to a people on earth. There has never been a more sacrilegious thing uttered by man, if it is not true. Now, I say, do you believe it? Do I believe it? I believe everything that has been revealed to the Prophet Joseph Smith. If any principle that has been revealed to the Prophet is not true, then it is all wrong, as far as I am concerned. There is no use of mincing over it.

Conference Report. April, 1909, p. 37.

No man was ever kinder to Golden Kimball than Lorenzo Snow. He put his arm around me before he died, and said, "I need you: I need your help; God bless you." That is the only time I have ever felt like a full grown man. I felt like I was eight feet tall, that God needed me. I have felt big only once, and that was the time when I thought God needed me in this great work.

Conference Report. April, 1910, p. 57.

I remember, in the early days of my youth, of the people of this Church looking forward hopefully when the time should come that the prophecy made by the servants of God would be fulfilled, *viz*: that President Joseph F. Smith would become the President of the Church of Jesus Christ of Latter-day Saints. I can think of no man who has been president of the Church, who has had greater opportunities and advantages than he has had. President Smith was chosen and ordained an apostle in his youth. He was favored, as I remember it, by being sent on a mission to the Hawaiian Islands, when he was 15 years old. He was hedged about and privileged in associating with great men, and his life and labors were in the service of the Lord, as a special witness and an apostle of Jesus Christ. President Smith was trained, instructed, and prepared for this great appointment as prophet, seer and revelator by the greatest men who ever lived, in my judgment, in the history of the world.

Conference Report. April, 1919, p. 23.

I have known President Grant and heard about him from his earliest childhood, for my mother was a very dear friend of his mother's and I have been in their home when I was a child. My own father, Heber C. Kimball, took him as a child, and stood him on a table and said:

"He will be an apostle," and it came true. Yes, I sustain President Grant with all my heart, for I realize in part at least, what a great responsibility rests upon him.

Conference Report. October, 1924, pp. 70-71.

I met a horny-handed son of toil the other day near the Church Office Building. He was a Scotchman, and said: "Brother Kimball, will you shake hands with me?" I said: "Yes, and be tickled to do it."

"Would you like to hear how I came to join the Church?"

"Yes, I would like to hear it, for I was born in the Church. I never knew anything else."

Then he told me his story. Little did that man know how he stimulated my faith just through that little friendship and testimony. As we stood there one of the brethren passed, in fact it was President Grant. My back was to him and I did not see him until after he got by. This Scotchman said: "Brother Kimball, as unbelievable as it is, I pray for that man twice every day of my life, and he did not speak to me."

"Well," I said, "he did not see you. President Grant cannot stop to shake hands with every man in all Israel and do anything else. You keep on praying, for he has a great responsibility resting upon him, for when he speaks in the name of God it is not his own word; it is the word of God...."

Conference Report. October, 1924, p. 71.

REPENTANCE

A man can't repent simply because an Apostle tells him to repent; he can't do it until he gets the spirit of repentance, which is a gift from God; and some of us don't get it very quickly. Some of us don't get the spirit of repentance and see things right until our hair is gray. Brethren, let us be tolerant; let us be kind and considerate.

Conference Report. April, 1908, pp. 117-118.

As my mother once said to my father, during the reformation, when he wanted her to repent, as all others were repenting, she said: "I am surprised that I have done as well as I have, and if I had it to do over again, I could not do as well." Father hardly thought that was repentance.

Conference Report. October, 1910, p. 32.

I acknowledge that I am imperfect, and no one is more sorry than I am. I have made mistakes, blunders, but I have faith in God, and I know God will forgive a man who repents.

Conference Report. April, 1913, p. 89.

REPUTATION

I remember something said once; I tried to forget it, but it went all over the land. It is the only time I ever did get any notoriety. (Laughter.) The grave question was, did he say it? I could not help but think of the young man who opened this meeting by prayer, of his own volition he got the signatures of eighteen men, intelligent men, business men, who signed a document to the effect that I did not say it. But the word had gone out that I did say it. Some of the brethren said, "Well, it sounded like him." Another good brother that wanted to help me out, said, "He did not say it, but he was not wise." That good brother killed me right there. (Laughter) You let it go out only once, among the children of men, that you are not wise, and you might just as well go off and die.

Conference Report. April, 1911, pp. 68-69.

SALVATION

My father, Heber, C. Kimball, once was discouraged and he said: "I do not know whether any of you will be saved. If any of you are saved I will be more surprised than anybody else."

Conference Report. April, 1938, p. 31.

I think it is wrong to despise the man that has a weakness, and make him feel that he is good for nothing, and that there is not much chance for him. I think I can safely say to you Latter-day Saints: You will all be saved, every one of you; the only difference will be this, some will be saved sooner than others. Every man that has transgressed and done wrong must pay the penalty of his transgression, for salvation costs something, and you have to pay the price or you don't get it.

Conference Report. April, 1908, p. 118.

SCRIPTURES

I am going to read to you a little that has been culled from the Bible as to the mission of Christ. I would quote it, but I never dare quote scripture, for after I get through quoting you wouldn't recognize it. I am a little like father, when he used to quote scripture, he would say, "Well, if that isn't in the Bible, it ought to be in it."

Conference Report. October, 1910, p. 32.

I find out some things by reading the Doctrine and Covenants—which, by the way, I do read. I am familiar with the Bible, a little, and the Book of Mormon, the Doctrine and Covenants and the Pearl of Great Price. I have wished, sometimes, that there would be a big fire and burn all the rest of the books so that we would read these books more. Sometimes I feel that a man ought to be imprisoned for writing any more books; because I got my experience mostly by reading the books which contain the revelations of the Lord. I got my first experience in the Southern states in two years, and I read the Bible; I read the Book of Mormon; and I read the Doctrine and Covenants and the Pearl of Great Price. I don't believe the man lives, unless God inspires him, who can ever breathe into a book what you can get out of the Bible, Book of Mormon, Doctrine and Covenants and Pearl of Great Price. That is my testimony.

Conference Report. October, 1921, p. 84.

In our associating among the people, we discovered and I want to testify to what one of the brethren spoke in reference to that matter, that our people are not a reading people, they do not diligently read the Bible, the Book of Mormon, and the Book of Doctrine and Covenants.

Conference Report. October, 1897, pp. 50-51.

Now, brethren, I do not want to say anything to hurt anyone's feelings about books that are written. I read the Bible through once, and when I got through I said: "I will never tackle it again in the flesh;" but I have read in it, and I am acquainted with it, and I have marked it. I would not give my Bible for all the Bibles in the world, because it is the only Bible I can find anything in.

Conference Report. October, 1921, p. 84.

I am strongly impressed with the idea that the Bible cannot be understood only by the same spirit with which it was written.

Conference Report. April, 1903, p. 31.

SELF IMAGE

We are one and all God's children. He created us and he never created a failure, and he created you.

Conference Report. October, 1937, p. 33.

Men come to me occasionally, not very often, and shake me by the hand and say, "I am glad to shake hands with a good man." I never feel so "cheap" as when that happens, and I have always been thankful that they did not know me so well as I know myself.

Conference Report. October, 1932, p. 17.

SERVICE

I am going to ask you a few questions, and will let you answer them. If you don't know enough to answer them, then you don't know as much as I do. I am going to ask you this question, Do you know of anything—you can think about your money, your wives, and children, and everything else—but do you know of anything in all this beautiful world more important than human life? If you do, just hold up your hands.

I am going to ask it in another way: "Do you know of anything in all this universe that is dearer to the Father than a human soul? You don't.

I am going to ask you another question: Do you know

of any gift in all this world, or blessing, that is greater than salvation? No, because God said in the revelation that "Salvation is the greatest gift of God to his children." These are reasons why you ought to be in the service of the Lord.

Conference Report. October, 1917, p. 135.

SIN

No single instance can be given as evidence that unlawful sensual pleasure can be indulged in without paying for it a thousand times in pain and remorse.

Conference Report. October, 1937, p. 32.

While I was in Venice, California, or Ocean Park, I saw three great battle-ships, the Wisconsin, the Tennessee and the California. I had the privilege of going on board the Tennessee. They left Venice on Friday morning at ten o'clock, and I saw those beautiful war vessels leave the harbor. I had not been on the pier long when I noticed a young man, called a jackie, one of the boys of the Tennessee. He was looking longingly over the ocean at those retreating ships. I asked him why he was not with the ships and he said: "I was fifteen minutes late." I asked him: "What will they do with you? What are you going to do? Why don't you take the railroad and run up to a station where they will stop, and get on your war vessel?" He said: "O, it don't make any difference, I will go down to San Pedro and get on the Dakota, and they will place me in chains and feed me on bread and water; but" said he, "I had a mighty good time." He had had a good time at Los Angeles, but he was fifteen minutes late, and according to his story he was to be disciplined, and he was to eat bread and water, and be placed in chains. I asked him what he did it for, and he said: "Well now, look here Mister, I did it and it is done, and I am trying to get a little sunshine out of this thing." That was a knockdown argument and I never said another word. If he could get any sunshine out of it I was willing for the poor fellow to have it.

Conference Report. April, 1908, p. 118.

Temptation somewhere in the life of all finds us, as this life is a testing time. Therefore, watch and pray and ask God to leave us not in temptation but deliver us from evil, and as temptation is ever lying in wait and in a thousand forms is temptation repeated.

Conference Report. October, 1926, p. 131.

SPEAKING

It takes lots of courage to say always what you think. The trouble is, we think things sometimes we ought not to say.

Conference Report. April, 1910, p. 53.

Arising to speak to you at this time puts me in mind of a story I read not long ago. It was during the late war, when some soldiers were around a camp fire, trying to keep themselves from freezing to death, a preacher came along to hold services. He looked around among the soldiers, and said, "I will take for my text Chilblains." So he instructed the soldiers what to do, which was to put soft soap in their shoes, place them on their feet and wait till their feet were healed, and then he would talk to them about the Lord the next time he came. You can't talk to people when they are uneasy, not if you are like I am. You can't preach to people when they want to go home. Now if any of you want to go, please go, and the rest of us will stay till we get through.

Conference Report. October, 1905, p. 81.

Horace Greeley used to say that the way to write a good editorial was to write it to the best of your ability, then cut it in two in the middle and print the last half. I am going to follow this suggestion.

Conference Report. April, 1923, p. 125.

Brethren and sisters, I have been thinking for quite a while about certain things, and I have been boiling it down, like my father used to boil down the sugar cane juice, until I have got it down to about what I want to say to you today.

Conference Report. October, 1912, p. 27.

It has been a fight all my life to follow men who have great ability and who were greatly blessed as public speakers. My lesson came to me in this way, that I discovered that no man was ever created that could reach all the people at one time, and I figured that there must be some poor soul with bowed head who was discouraged and disheartened to whom I might, through the blessings of the Lord, and under the influence of his Holy Spirit, give a word of cheer....

Conference Report. October, 1926, p. 127.

I remember that not many Conferences ago I was called to the stand just before the Conference adjourned. President Grant told me I had seven minutes—I took three—and I think it is the only time that President

Grant ever shook hands with me after one of my talks. President Grant did not shake hands with me because of what I said; it was because I had left him four minutes, and that is more than any of the other brethren had ever done.

Conference Report. April, 1932, p. 77.

To begin with, I came to this meeting prepared to speak, expecting to speak; and came provided with some information. Having done my part, the rest depends upon the Lord, and His Spirit, and the attention that I receive from the people.

Conference Report. April, 1910, p. 52.

A little fellow was sick and he went to the doctor who was a herbalist. The doctor gave him four herbs and told him to boil them in a quart of water and drink it all. The little fellow said: "I can't. I only hold a pint." I am wondering how much you people hold?

Conference Report. April, 1929, p. 127.

I am very desirous that I may have your attention as well as your faith and prayers for a short time.

Conference Report. October, 1899, p. 53.

I am ready to confess that I am keyed up to a pretty high tension, and the only thing I am afraid of is that I will say just what I think, which would be unwise, no doubt.

Conference Report. April, 1904, p. 28.

STEWARDSHIP

I don't think there is anything in this Church to be done that I can't do, if the proper authorities tell me to do it, but there are many things they don't tell me to do, so I let it alone. It has taken me a long time to learn to mind my own business. . . .

Conference Report. April, 1908.

STUDY

The effects of idleness and mental laziness cause a stupor of thought and will grieve the spirit of the Lord, and if persisted in will result in the withdrawal of the Spirit of the Lord.

Conference Report. October, 1901, p. 57.

I believe there was a time in the history of this church when it was necessary to send all kinds of men! God magnified them, and made them marvelous; but I tell you He does not look upón ignorance now with any degree of allowance. There is no need of our Priesthood being ignorant; there is no need of our Priesthood going out as the fishermen went out. They ought to go out well equipped and fitted for the work of the Lord as special witnesses of Christ. I know what the Lord wants in this respect, just as well as if He gave me a direct revelation.

Conference Report. October, 1905, p. 83.

We believe that men who are aged should study just as much as young men. I want to ask the Latter-day Saints if that is a true doctrine, that when a man gets old he should quit learning and stop studying, and cease to progress.

Conference Report. October, 1897, p. 51.

We have seen men handled because they waded into mysteries, and, of course, it was proper and right when they waded into mysteries and preached false doctrines that they should be handled. I can see the righteousness of it, but I wonder if any man has ever been handled in the kingdom of God for not knowing anything. I am in favor of some of them being handled right away.

Conference Report. April, 1901, p. 62.

To get a true conception of God is the biggest idea I have ever tried to comprehend.

Conference Report. April, 1923, p. 126.

SUCCESS

Any man who tries to do the right thing and continues to try, is not a failure in the sight of God.

Conference Report. April, 1907, p. 82.

TALENTS

As much as I honor and respect Brother Roberts I have never felt inferior to him in his presence; he has never made me feel that way. He had a greater intellect, greater intelligence, but I have had some gifts of my own, that in a way were equal to his. I have preached by his side many times, and after he got through preaching I reached those that he missed, so it has been that way during all this time.

Conference Report. October, 1933, p. 43.

TEMPLE

It is part of the vision that Brigham Young saw. Think of the temple! When Brigham Young struck his cane in the ground and said: "Right here we will build a temple to our God;" it was in the time of their poverty when they were so poor that father came along when the men working on the temple were soaking their bread in the stream of water. Father said: "To you it will be the sweetest bread in all your life." It took forty years to build that temple. I will never forget when it was dedicated. I was in the Southern States where they were driving us like wild animals, and we took our lives in our hands. I heard that prophet say when the temple was dedicated, as I was here on a visit: "From this time forth the hearts of the children of men will be softened towards us." I stand before you as a witness of the softening of the hearts of the people in the south. See what has been accomplished.

Conference Report. October, 1924, p. 72.

TESTIMONY

I am fearful that some of the Latter-day Saints simply come to the leaders and listen to the servants of God, and they never study it out in their minds; they never go to the written word, and compare it with the servants of God in their doctrines and teachings, and consequently they are unable to judge righteously, and they are losing confidence. Their confidence is being shaken, and they are unable to judge, because they have not first studied it out in their minds, because, as a people, we are mentally lazy.

Conference Report. October, 1897, p. 51.

I am not a visionary man, I am not a dreamer. I sometimes wonder what my gift is. I have never seen an angel, but I have the assurance that comes to me and is burned in my heart like a living fire by the power of the Holy Ghost, that God is the Father, that Jesus is the Christ.

Conference Report. October, 1932, p. 20.

I am verging on my eighty-second year. I have the same living testimony today that I had when I began this work. I have the same testimony that I had when I stood in Virginia proclaiming the Gospel of Jesus Christ to the people just fifty years ago. I am telling you good people I have had a full life of experience, having a wife and six children, with all life's joys, struggles, hardships and sacrifices. I am telling you plainly and frankly that the greatest joy, the greatest peace, and the greatest happiness I have ever had in my life have come when speaking under the spirit of testimony. I have felt that thrill throughout my being. It is a joy and happiness that cannot be expressed.

Conference Report. April, 1935, p. 35.

I am a son of a prophet, but I never got my knowledge and information from my father. I expect to get it from the same sources from which he received it; and if I live as close to God as he lived, I will have the same knowledge of God as he had, and know that Jesus is the Christ.

Conference Report. April, 1911, p. 69.

I have been thinking, not only today, but during this conference of a testimony that my father bore when he was fifty-four years old, and it gives me a great deal of pleasure to know that I am now fifty-three years of age and have the same testimony that he had—not one whit's difference; that I have a knowledge of the truth of the Gospel. I have been taught it from my youth, just as I was taught in early days that a peach grew on a peach tree. I believe I have just as much knowledge of a peach now as the most scientific man in the world. I can tell a peach when I see it, and a peach tree; but I cannot for the life of me tell how that peach grows on a peach tree, and neither can you. Now, there are many things about this work that I do not comprehend, but because I cannot tell it all it does not prove that it is not true.

85

Conference Report. October, 1906, p. 117.

I think many of the Latter-day Saints are greatly frightened. You don't know what is going to happen. Time must be close at hand when we shall need a living testimony and knowledge for ourselves that God lives and that Jesus Christ is the Savior of the world.

Conference Report. April, 1923, p. 127.

TITHING

Some of these men get in debt, and a few of them have told me that the Lord is so merciful and their creditors are so hard on them that they will pay them first.

Conference Report. April, 1903, p. 33.

TRIALS

I feel more like saying, this morning, "Cheer up, the worst is to come."

Conference Report. October, 1931, p. 55.

What is in the future? How far can we see ahead of us? Some of us cannot see the length of our noses, but the prophets have warned us of the danger that menaces us. We must be prepared and get our feet planted upon the ground, because we don't know, I don't know, what test is ahead of us.

Conference Report. April, 1923, p. 126.

You have to knock some "Mormons" down every little while to keep them in the Church. It is too bad, but we as Latter-day Saints cannot be prospered without some of us getting arrogant and proud and forgetting God.

Conference Report. April, 1926, p. 60.

TRUTH

All great men have been misunderstood. So I conclude that to be misunderstood is greatness; that is, if you speak the truth.

Conference Report. October, 1925, p. 155.

UTAH

I have heard from time to time, since our last conference, some who were non-"Mormons," some who were non-residents of Utah, and some of our own rising generation, speak very lightly about what President Brigham Young said when he entered this valley, "This is the place." Well, I am here to say it is the place, and 'I just came from California, too.

Conference Report. April, 1924, p. 69.

Brethren and sisters, I know we have had a great deal of praise. I have been deeply interested in what has been said—that we are the best people on earth. But a short time ago, a brother of mine, whom you know, a humble man at the wicker gate of the temple block, went down to Los Angeles to look around and see what the prospects were, as he was given a vacation. He is a gardener and a great lover of flowers, and he has helped beautify a great many places here in the city. He was working for a great florist down there in Los Angeles, and they sent him to a multi-millionaire's home, and he worked there six weeks. This wealthy man came out and talked to him. Kimball had no fear and told him he was a "Mormon." The man looked at him and said: "Well, I am awfully glad to have a 'Mormon' work on my place." Kimball told him he was a son of Heber C. Kimball. The man said, "Do you know that those old men, (that is the way he phrased it) Brigham Young, and Heber C. Kimball and those pioneers were the greatest people on earth, and we love to have"—he was speaking generally of the "Mormon" and Gentile—"these Utah people come down here, because they are honest, because we can trust them."

Conference Report. April, 1925, p. 120.

I think it was on the 6th of March that I preached to the people of the Latter-day Saint branch in San Francisco. When I finished, the presiding officer said: "Brother Kimball, if you preach another sermon like that about Utah, all the people will leave." That makes clear how much I think of Utah and her people.

Conference Report. October, 1924, p. 70.

WISDOM

I am trying to be wise, and I am trying to be prudent, and I confess to you I am having a terrible time.

Conference Report. April, 1908, p. 116.

It is considered a good thing to look wise, especially when not over burdened with information.

Conference Report. April, 1906, p. 74.

WOMEN

If I have ever been vain—and no doubt I have been—I think men are really more vain than women, and that is a hard blow!

Conference Report. April, 1927, p. 52.

WORK

Construction is very difficult, destruction is easy.

Conference Report. October, 1906, p. 117.

I pray the Lord that He may move upon all of us that are in need of assistance, that we will have the pride of a Latter-day Saint, and not receive anything when we are able to work, unless we be furnished employment. That demand should be made upon the Latter-day Saints, and I felt impressed that if the time ever came that I had no food for my family, I would go among the Latter-day Saints and as a servant of God I would demand work. And if you would not give me work the Lord would take from the abundance which you are blessed with.

Conference Report. April, 1898, p. 44.

YOUTH

We are a good deal like Peter. I was that way. I would have cut more than one of their ears off, if there had been someone to stick them on again. That is the spirit of young men at first; but after awhile they moderate.

Conference Report. April, 1902, p. 9.

I remember being in a far-off settlement not long ago, where they see few if any of the leading brethren, and yet they number over twelve hundred. They have a great many young people, and when I retired to my bed after the meeting I was kept awake all night long by the boys and girls running the streets of that settlement. I got up towards morning, looked at my watch, and it was then 4 a.m., and they were still roaming the streets. While it may have been harmless and they may have been pure in their intentions, I tell you in the name of Israel's God it is one of the criminal things that are going on in this land. The devil is breathing in the hearts of our young people, and the very air is stagnated in some of our larger cities with the spirit of immorality, and no greater sin can find its way in the hearts of our young people.

Conference Report. April, 1902, pp. 10-11.

ZION

Now, Zion will be redeemed, and I want to say to you, my brethren and sisters, that all is not well in Zion; but if you wish to be popular you want to say that all is well in Zion.

Conference Report. April, 1898, p. 44.

BIOGRAPHICAL DATA

1853   On June 9, Jonathan Golden Kimball was born in the Kimball Mansion on North Main Street. His parents were Heber C. Kimball and Christeen Golden Kimball.

1868   Heber C. Kimball died. J. Golden quit school and became a mule skinner to support his mother, younger brother Elias, and sister Mary Margaret. He later became a contractor whose business included freighting, excavating, hauling rock, and other work requiring teams.

1876   Upon the failure of the contracting business   the Kimballs moved to Meadowville, Rich County, four miles from Bear Lake. J. Golden and Elias bought squatter's claims from Isaac and Solomon Kimball for $1000. This was the first time they had gone into debt. Eventually their ranch became one of the most successful in the Bear Lake area.

1881   J. Golden and Elias heard Karl G. Maeser speak in Meadowville and became determined to go to the Brigham Young Academy and make something of themselves. To finance their schooling they sold washing machines. Their mother accompanied them to Provo and J. Golden attended B.Y.A. for two years.

1883   On April 6, J. Golden Kimball received a call to the Southern States Mission. After the first year of his mission he served as the mission secretary to B. H. Roberts. It was during the last year of his mission that he contracted malaria which was the beginning of the physical problems which plagued him the rest of his life.

1887   J. Golden married Jennie Knowlton. They eventually parented six children: Jonathan, Quince, Elizabeth, Gladys, Richard, and Max. The family moved to Logan at this time and J. Golden and Elias sold farm implements and speculated on property near Logan.

1891   J. Golden Kimball was called as President of the Southern States Mission.

1892   J. Golden was called as one of the first Presidents of the Council of the Seventy. At this time they sold the ranch in Meadowville.

1894   He was released from his mission and returned home.

1896   J. Golden was called to be an aid to the Young Men's Mutual Improvement Association.

1900-1922   J. Golden served not only as one of the First Presidents of the Council of the Seventy but also as office secretary to the First Council of the Seventy.

1938   On September 2, J. Golden Kimball died in a car accident near Reno, Nevada. The speakers at his large funeral included Heber J. Grant, George Albert Smith, and David O. McKay.